3-1821
8X 6
10120

Jesus Christ:

PROPHET PRIEST

By
Andrew Murray

BETHANY FELLOWSHIP, INC.
MINNEAPOLIS, MINNESOTA

PREFACE

With the humble prayer that our great Prophet may use these simple words to teach His people the truth concerning himself and His blessed work, I send my loving greetings in Him to all into whose hands the little book may come.

Andrew Murray

CONTENTS

HISTORIC NOTE

These four addresses were delivered by the Rev. Andrew Murray, of Wellington, South Africa, at the Mildmay Conference of 1895.

As this little book may find its way to all parts of the world, and as Mr. Murray, in his warm introduction, makes special allusion to the "gatherings of the saints of God at Mildmay," it may be desirable to refer to the origin of these conferences.

They were commenced at Barnet, near London, in 1856, by the Rev. W. and Mrs. Pennefather, who longed for the manifestation of true Christian union; and they were continued when he became Vicar of St. Jude's, Mildmay Park.

Mildmay is therefore the mother of the many conferences of believers which are now convened all over the world.

CHAPTER ONE

THE LORD JESUS CHRIST:
Our Prophet

PROPHET, PRIEST, KING

Fulness of prophetic story,
    Fulness filling all in all;
Brightness of the hidden glory,
    Answer to the world's long call—
Jesus, Thou our future knowest,
    Fill it with Thyself alone;
May we follow where Thou goest,
    Ever Thee our Prophet own.

Great High Priest, above all other,
    Sacrifice of God complete,
May we never own another,
    Or confess at other feet;
Never seek another altar,
    Never wish another Lamb,
Pardoned, washed, why should we falter,
    Pleading in Thy priestly name?

King of kings! may Thy dominion
    Multiply and still increase;
Give Thy sway the eagle's pinion,
    King of Righteousness and Peace.
Rule within Thy Church! inherit
    All that Thou hast bought, great Son;
Rule o'er each blood-ransomed spirit,
    Prophet, Priest, and King in one.

                       —William Luff

"A prophet is a spokesman of God—one who does not speak at his own will, one who does not utter his own sentiments, but who speaks the words that God gives him to speak (Jer. 23:22). That was the work of a prophet—to stand in the Cabinet of Jehovah and make the people hear His words. God was the speaker and the prophets were but the mouthpiece of God."
—J. G. McVicker

"The Lord Jesus Christ was God's spokesman to us, the manifestation of God to us. I have been amazed, over and over again, to read that the Lord Jesus Christ never uttered a word of His own. I have had to read it again and again, and I have often turned to see if it is really there, but there it is. In John 12:49 it is written, 'The Father gave me a commandment, what I should say, and what I should speak.' Just think of it. Some of us want to be original, and say something original, to pray something original, to think out something original. Oh! how ashamed we ought to be of ourselves if such a thought ever took possession of us for a moment, when the Lord Jesus was, as we understand it, never original. The Father told Him always what to say. Yes, remember John 12:49, and forget not John 14:10, for there we read that the Lord said that the words He spoke He spoke not of himself; but the Father, who dwelt in Him, He did the works."—Pastor D. M. Stearns, D.D.

Let us read from the three first verses of Hebrews chapter 1. "God hath in these last days spoken unto us by his Son...; who, when he had by himself purged our sins, sat down on the right hand of the Majesty on high."

You see that in these three verses we have the three offices of Christ. "God hath ... spoken ... by his Son": that is the prophetic office; "who, when he had purged our sins": that is the priestly office; "sat down on the right hand of [God]": that is the kingly office. The three are inseparably united in just the order in which they are given here. I want, by God's help, to help you and myself to understand what it means, that I have a Prophet in Him. The Church has Christ as its Prophet, and so do I.

Notice the close connection between these three offices. It is not accidental that there are three offices, and not two, nor four; but it is, in the very nature of things, just what we need. Man has in his nature three great faculties: the power of knowing, the power of feeling, and the power of willing.

First of all, I *know*—that is, I am aware of the things that are outside of me; I have a sense by which I can take cognizance of them. I can see when it is dark or light, whether a man is standing yonder or not; I know.

Secondly, I *feel*. Light or darkness makes a pleasant or unpleasant impression: I feel happy or unhappy; I feel good or evil.

Then there is the third: I can *will*. When I

know a thing, I can desire it. When it affects me pleasantly I can choose it.

And now, just as there are these three powers in the human soul, so God meets us with this threefold work of grace.

Sin destroys all the three faculties. My understanding, my power of knowing, has been darkened. My feeling, my consciousness of what I am, brings me nothing but wretchedness and a sense of condemnation. Then my will has been perverted: I choose the evil.

Christ meets these three needs of my being. As Prophet, He brings the light of God into my heart. He reveals to me my sin and wretchedness; that is the first thing He shows in the light of God. However, He tells me not only my sin but God's love, too, and the way to God! He tells me God has made Him a Priest to bring me nigh to Him. And shining into my heart as a Prophet, He brings me to His priestly work of redeeming, purging, and sanctifying, and teaches me to understand that. You see the Prophet first, and then the Priest. Then comes the kingly office. As King, He fits me to rule over sin and self.

Therefore, do not look upon the three offices of Christ as something accidental but understand how inseparable they are.

Try also to take hold of the truth that the prophetic office must come first. I am afraid that there is a great tendency to exalt the priestly office above the prophetic, and then the kingly office above the prophetic too. I am persuaded the Church suffers immense damage from that. Just lately I read in a well-known theological work that the priesthood is of "super-eminent importance." I do not believe it. Do not think that I do not adore and worship Christ as our ever-blessed Melchizedek; but the prophetic office must be as precious as the priestly office.

Let me first remind you how the prophetic office always precedes. Look at it in history. Moses was the great prophet of whom God said, "I will raise up one like unto him." There you have the prophet first, then came Aaron the priest; later on you read of the king. In the life of Jesus it is the same; for three years He acted as Prophet, teaching; then on Calvary began the priestly office; and with the ascension began the kingship. The prophet must prepare the way.

Now you can see why it is that the Church can suffer harm if she neglects the prophetic office of Christ. The prophetic office is the gate to the priestly and kingly offices. How am I to enjoy the blessings of the priest and king unless I have the prophet to enlighten me and lead me up and teach me to take possession of what God has prepared.

Oh, friends! what is the reason that so many who have a strong faith in the priesthood of Christ—praise God for that wonderful priesthood!—so often complain, "I do not realize His power. I believe in the blood, and I believe in a living High Priest, and I believe in the Holiest of all opened for me; but somehow it has no power over me. Why does it not influence my heart and life more?" It is simply because you take that truth more from the Church than from Jesus himself; by study and thought from the teaching of your mother, or your minister, or your Bible; and you do not allow the Holy Spirit himself, as the gift of our divine Prophet, to lead you into the blessed mysteries of divine truth.

It is not enough to have a priest and a king; there must be a prophet. In the spiritual life there is not a more practical truth for me than this: I must have Jesus as a Prophet. He is the Prophet of whom God said, "Hear him"—not now and then; no! but every day and every hour. My soul rejoices that it is Jesus the Prophet who will reveal to me Jesus the High Priest and lead me on through the blood to the kingship. Let us beware of accounting this prophetic office of Christ a little thing. Let us beware of limiting it to the future—the prophecies in regard to the future. No, as we have already heard, the Prophet is, in all things, the mouthpiece of God—not only One who foretells, but One who tells us how to live.

Let me say one thing more to illustrate the truth that the prophetic office has been neglected. Do we not all thank God unceasingly for the blessed Reformation, when the great truth was proclaimed that a man needs no intervention of a fellowman in drawing near to God; but that every anxious soul can go straight to God, because the High Priest lives and is accessible to everyone? Tell me, has the great truth that I need no intervention between Christ and me, as Prophet, that I can be directly taught by the Holy Ghost, been equally acknowledged and proclaimed?

Tell me, from your experience and the teaching you have heard, whether the prophetic honor of Jesus has been maintained as His priestly glory has. I think not. We have not honored Jesus the Prophet as we should have done. You know the great difference—I find it difficult to express it in words—but the great difference between the prophetic office and the priestly and kingly offices was this: The priestly and kingly offices were in Israel a fixed institution. All the children of Aaron, down the ages, were priests. Just so with the kings, the sons of David. They were the royal race; however wretched and ungodly they might have been, it was a fixed thing. But there was no race of prophets. The prophets were raised up by God from time to time. Just when priesthood and kingship had failed and dishonored God, then were the prophets raised up.

In the prophetic office there is more directness of divine interposition, a dependence upon God's immediate and ever-renewed operation, with a liberty of action and progressiveness, than there is in the priestly and kingly offices. Hence it is far easier for us to get a clear comprehension of the priestly and kingly offices. The priestly office gives access to God. It deals with a finished work. Just so with the kingly office: Christ is sat down upon the throne. The prophetic office is far more difficult of apprehension. It implies that I

11

must, day by day, in the confession of ignorance, in docility and dependence, wait upon the heavenly teaching. It implies that each time I read one word of God's precious Word, I must ask God to let the divine Prophet speak into my ear. It implies a continuous, direct, personal relationship with God. The glory of the prophetic office has not been understood. The belief in priesthood and kingship has not exercised a sanctifying effect because we have not waited upon Christ by the Spirit to reveal to us what the priesthood and kingship give.

Let us now go further and see what the way is in which Christ exercises this prophetic office. Have you ever observed that in the last night when Christ spoke those wonderful chapters, John 14 to 17, and gave the promise of the Holy Spirit, the chief thing that He said about the Holy Spirit is something which is not ordinarily placed first? We generally think of two things in connection with the Holy Spirit: holiness, or sanctification, and power for service. But what the Lord Jesus Christ especially emphasized and repeated was this: "The Spirit will guide you into all truth." That was with Jesus the chief thought.

Ah, friends, is there not too much of our religion that is without this divine teaching, because we have not known our blessed Prophet, the One who teaches us each day? Let me just quote from St. Paul something that will illustrate this.

You remember in the first Epistle to the Corinthians, where Paul was telling them of Christ sending him to teach, he writes that when Christ sent him, He gave him one warning—that he must preach the Gospel, but not with man's wisdom or he would make the cross of Christ of none effect. He did not say, "Paul, take care you preach the cross," but He said, "Take care, when you do preach, that you do not rely on man's wisdom."

Then in chapter 2 Paul goes on to tell us, "I came not with excellency of speech, or of wisdom," because Christ is the wisdom of God. You know how he had taught in chapter 1 that Christ has been made unto us wisdom, righteousness, sanctification, and complete redemption.

Brothers and sisters, I do ask all of you who have accounted that text in I Corinthians 1 a precious jewel, has not the thought, "Christ is my righteousness," been far more precious than "Christ is my wisdom"? And that ought not to be. If we knew what it is to bow in deep humility and set aside all human wisdom, and to seek to be freed from the power of beautiful words, simply waiting for the Holy Ghost to teach, there would be new power in the preaching. Christ, as Prophet, does His work by the Holy Spirit.

But what is now the work of the prophet? In the Old Testament you will find the prophet has three things to do. One is to convince of sin. God raised up Elijah and Elisha, Isaiah and

13

Jeremiah, Ezekiel, and all the prophets, to testify against the sins of Israel. "Cry aloud, and spare not. Shew my people their transgression." That is the work of the prophet.

The second work is that he reveals the spiritual truth and law of God. The prophets had to reveal what the spiritual meaning of sacrifice was, what the spiritual meaning of the temple service and religion was, what the spiritual meaning of prayer was. They had not only to convict of sin but to teach all the truth of God.

The third thing they had to do was to convey promises in regard to the future (sometimes in the near and immediate future)—promises of deliverance from the hand of enemies; promises of God's presence in the midst of His people. They were to awaken a holy expectancy.

Oh, brothers, is not the Church of Christ in our day just in need of this prophetic work of Christ? You know how He does it. He does it by men upon earth. You have read about Aaron being a prophet to Moses. Yes, and Christ is the revealer of the heart of the Father—of God's holiness, of His love, of His saving power. Would that God would raise up to us prophets to testify against the worldliness and sin of His people!

I remember years ago getting a letter from a missionary in Africa, and he said, "Would that God would raise up prophets in this world!" When every minister learns to wait upon Him as His mouthpiece, depend upon it, God will give the needful prophets and needful power to testify against sin. It is the work of Jesus

14

through the Holy Ghost. Once again we need to have the spirituality of our religion revealed as the prophets did it of old.

When the priesthood and kingship, in times of decay, had fallen into disrepute, the prophets came to call men back again. We have taken the truths we hold too little from Jesus Christ himself; this is the reason they have not more spiritual power in our life. But let our hearts be glad. Christ is able and willing to restore every spiritual truth of God. That truth which we sometimes misapprehend and sometimes rob of its spiritual power, Christ is able to make a reality in our very hearts.

It is the work of the prophet thus to convince of sin and to reveal the spiritual truth of God; but above all, it is his work to awaken a holy expectancy. Praise God, there are not a few who, when they look upon the state of Christendom, feel that we can do nothing, and yet they dare look up and believe that with God there is deliverance; their whole spirit is that of waiting upon God and hoping in Him.

Oh, brothers, if you want your hearts awakened to cheerful confidence and expectancy, honor Christ the Prophet. He will show you what God can do, is going to do. Once again Christ Jesus is the mouthpiece of God to show us all that God is preparing to do for us.

I have spoken of what Christ does. Now comes the practical application. What is He to be to us? Here I have just two thoughts. First, in regard to the Church in general—oh, let us all pray without ceasing for the Church of Christ, that the prophetic honor and office of Christ may be acknowledged in its full glory. I say it again: we all rejoice that in our Protestant Christendom, there is no more thought of a priest intervening between our souls and God; Christ himself sprinkles us with the blood. We may, indeed, have direct communion with God. It is not otherwise with the teaching and guidance Jesus gives. Let us pray to God that in the work of the Church this blessed truth may be brought forth in its fullness, that everyone may have direct contact with Jesus—not only the saving Jesus, the redeeming Jesus, but also the teaching Jesus.

Let us pray, too, that God will give to all of His ministers of the gospel, all faithful preachers of the gospel, a right sense of their holy position. Christ, the mouthpiece of God; I, the mouthpiece of Christ. You, my brother ministers, servants of God, and you workers all, men and women, who love to tell of Jesus in your Sunday schools or elsewhere—I pray you, if you are to honor Jesus as the Prophet, as the mouthpiece of God, then you must live toward Him as He lived toward God. You must give yourselves to prayer in continuous waiting, in quiet self-abnegation and trust, to be taught by himself through the Spirit. Christ the Prophet will use you as perhaps He has never done.

My second thought is a word to all individual believers. Beloved, it will have profited us very little to have heard about Christ, the burden and

16

fulfillment of the prophetic word, if we are content to have only the thought of what the word prophesied in the past, and how it has been fulfilled. We need something more: we need the living Christ himself. Christ's installation as Prophet was beside the Jordan when He was baptized, and the words were heard, "This is my beloved Son." So, listen to Jesus, the living One. "Hear ye him." That is it. Christ, our heavenly Prophet, can descend and come down into our whole life. With every spiritual perplexity we feel, with every prayer we send up, with every difficulty in our daily path, He can be our Teacher.

Let Jesus be your Prophet, let Him be your Teacher. Wait on Him: "They that wait on the Lord shall never be ashamed." Above all, if you are longing that He should lead you into the mysteries and blessedness of the priesthood into the very Holiest of all within the veil, there ever to dwell in God's light—if you would have Him lead you into the faith, the experience and the joy of the ransomed, and enable you to sing every day, "Now unto him who loved us, and washed us from our sins in his own blood, and ... made us ... priests unto God," then let Jesus, as the Prophet, come in. Bow before Him even now, yield yourself to Him, rejoice in Him, and trust Him.

" 'No man hath ascended up to heaven but he that came down from heaven, even the Son of man who is in heaven.' That is to say, all other human prophets have been, as it were, trying to reach up to heaven, and directly they have got to the mountain height, and God has given them a direct revelation of His truth, they have come down again and made known that revelation. But no man has ascended up to heaven to get the whole revelation, save He who came down from heaven. This is why the Lord Jesus Christ is a true Prophet—because He is the Son. In John 1:18, we read, 'No man hath seen God at any time; the only begotten Son which is in the bosom of the Father, he hath declared him,' and it is because He is the Son of God, because He was in the bosom of the Father, therefore, He is that Prophet that should come into the world."—Rev. E. A. Stuart

CHAPTER TWO

THE LORD JESUS CHRIST:

The Completion of Priesthood

"What a wonderful Saviour the Lord Jesus Christ is! Each new glimpse that we get of His glory seems to be brighter and better than anything we have ever seen before; and when He comes to do any new work of grace in our hearts, it seems the very best that He can do for us. So, when we hear of our Lord Jesus Christ as the Prophet, we are tempted to exclaim, 'Surely this is His most wonderful office! Surely there can be nothing in Christ that goes higher or is more glorious than His work of revealing God the Father!' When we turn to speak of Him as the Priest, we cry, 'God forbid that I should glory, save in the cross of the Lord Jesus Christ.' And when we see Him as our King, we fall in adoration at His feet, and crown Him Lord of all. So we need to be reminded that we must not set any one of these offices against the other, for the whole Jesus is fully in each of them.

"But our subject now is the priestly work of the Lord Jesus; and what I would say to you, dear friends, is this: Give yourselves up for a while to the adoration of our Lord Jesus as Priest. Be content, for the time being, to think of this as His most wonderful work; and ask God that afresh the glory of it may break in upon your soul."—Rev. G. H. C. MacGregor

Let us read the first verse of the eighth chapter of Hebrews. "Now of the things which we have spoken this is the sum [the Revised Version says 'this is the chief point']: We have such an High Priest who is set on the right hand of the throne of the Majesty in the heavens" —Jesus Christ, the completion of sacrifice and priesthood.

What is the object of priesthood? It is the restoration of fellowship with God. The priest was to take the sinner into God's presence. Religion. What is that? We have just as much of religion as we have of God. The increase of religion, the revival of religion, means nothing but this: to get more of God into our hearts and lives, and more of God's will, more of God's presence, more of God's power.

Priesthood means simply this: the bringing of us into perfect fellowship with God. See how this is illustrated in the story of Israel. Look at Exodus 25:8, just where God begins to give Moses His command about the tabernacle and the priesthood. He has spoken of the freewill offerings, and then follows, "Let them make me a sanctuary; that I may dwell among them." God wanted to live near, to live with, to live among His people. He wanted His people to live with and near Him. Look at chapter 29. There we have it more distinctly connected with priesthood. In verses 44 and 45 we read: "I will sanctify also both Aaron and his sons, to minister to me in the priest's office; and I will dwell among the children of Israel, and will be their God." Priesthood has no object apart from God's dwelling among His people.

And now in the New Testament, the great object of the priesthood is this: that we may dwell with God every hour of our lives and that God may dwell with us and in us. Dear friends, it is well that we should ever go back to Calvary and the atonement, to the Cross and the precious blood, to look at the everlasting foundation of our hope. When, however, a man has laid a foundation, he does not always abide there; but up and up and higher up he builds, until the superstructure is complete. Calvary and the Cross are our foundation. But what is now the house that God has built upon that? What is now the life into which God leads us through the Cross and Calvary? If we study all that the priesthood implies, we shall have the answer to that question.

Let me speak to you first of all about Jesus himself—the High Priest. Everything must commence there. Then we can go on to see a little of His work as High Priest in heaven; and after that, what that work will accomplish for us in the world.

We look first at Jesus. And what is it that constitutes Him such a perfect High Priest? You know how the Epistle to the Hebrews tells of that. It consists in this: that He is God and that He is man. As God, He is the omnipotent Creator—not only holy and righteous and able to conquer sin outside of us, but as Creator-God He has access to our inmost being, so that He can indeed cleanse us and lift these hearts of ours into fellowship with God. And then, He is not only God, but He is man. We see in that beautiful fifth chapter the two great thoughts connected with His humanity. One, that He himself was perfected in obedience by His suffering and His struggle. He learned obedience; and so, as our High Priest, He can teach us obedience. And when He, as High Priest, gives us His Holy Spirit, the Spirit that He gives us is the very Spirit of the obedience that was in Him. Let us take that in.

The very essence of Christ's work on Calvary is obedience to God. He gave himself up to the will of another—not His own will, but the will of His Father. And when Christ, as Priest, brings me up to God, it is by the divine Spirit that He puts into me, and He gives me the same mind and disposition as was in Him.

Then there is the other thought: We see in His humanity the deep tenderness with which He sank down into perfect conformity with us, into all our tears and prayers and sufferings. And therefore I may have great confidence that there is no place in which I am and no condition in which I suffer but that the High Priest is willing to enter into its depths, to make himself one with me, and in it and out of it to lift me up to God.

Oh, brother! my Christ is God! Mystery of mysteries! My Christ is man—a man as I myself am. The Epistle to the Hebrews tells how Christ as man, having finished the sacrifice for us, went up to heaven and now has a heavenly priesthood. There He carries on the priesthood in divine and everlasting power. It is the heavenly priesthood of Christ we want to think of. This is the sum of all that is written here and throughout God's Gospel. "We have such an High Priest who is set down at the right hand of the throne of the Majesty on high." Christ is a heavenly High Priest who gives us a heavenly life and enables us to lead a heavenly life on earth.

And now, what is the work that He does as this great High Priest? He brings us nigh unto God. In connection with that, there is a double work of which this eighth chapter of Hebrews speaks. If you read this chapter carefully, you will find that Christ there bears two names: the one name is the "Minister of the Sanctuary"; the other, the "Mediator of the Covenant." These two names are linked together inseparably. And it is just these two that we need.

What do I understand when I find that word, "the minister of the sanctuary"? In every temple there was a god, an unseen god, to whom the temple was devoted. But there was a priest, the priest of that temple, who was to receive the petitions or the sacrifices of the worshipper and to get the answer back from God. So it was with Aaron. It is said of him and of the priests in Israel, "they shall stand in my presence to minister," and "they shall go out and bless in my name."

There is a Godward and a manward redemption. And so Jesus stands as the Minister of the Sanctuary in His Godward work; and He stands as the Mediator of the Covenant, especially in

23

His manward work. What does that mean? Christ, as the Minister of the Sanctuary, has done these things: First of all, He opened the sanctuary. This He did by His blood. When He ascended into heaven He entered, with His own blood, into the Holiest place. And we read that with that blood, with that sacrifice—the better sacrifice—the heavenly things were all cleansed, and that in opening the Holiest with His blood, He secured us complete and most confident access into God's presence. He is the Minister of the Sanctuary.

But He is more. He lives there that He may ever act for us, do the work of bearing us up before the Father. He prays. It is written, "He liveth to pray." These are prayers not with words, prayers not such as ours; but His whole being, His presence before God, is one unceasing intercession. Without ceasing there rises from Him to the Father a cry that never fails, a cry for more spirit, and more life, and more blessing, and more of the love of God to be manifested in the Church of Christ here on earth. And without interruption, there flows back from the Father to the Son, in whom He delights, a stream of blessing to impart to His Body upon earth.

And even so, there flows forth unceasingly from the Son a stream of blessing unto His believing people. It is flowing even now. Do try and realize this. Just as the sun does not exist for one moment without pouring out its light, so our Lord Jesus cannot exist—I say it with reverence—cannot exist one single moment without the love and Spirit and power and blessing of God flowing out from Him. If we did but learn to believe in the power of that intercession, what lives should we live, and with what joy would we sing, "To him that loveth us, and loosed us from our sins by his blood; . . . to him be the glory and the dominion"!

Now, the Priest not only opened the temple, and He not only dwells there as an intercessor— He does more. He brings us in. He has told us in His Word that we all are to live in the Holiest of all. You know the text, "Having therefore, brethren, boldness to enter into the holiest, . . . let us draw nigh." Alas! our hearts are so foolish, so feeble, and so ready to fail that we too often think, "I cannot enter into that holy place, and I never could expect to be always kept abiding there. How could I, with this sinful nature, always, without ceasing, live in the house of God, in the presence of the thrice Holy One?"

Here comes the blessed thought to help us: Christ is the Minister of the Sanctuary. He is there to take thee in, to bring thee in, to keep thee in, to bring thee ever deeper in. He is there to watch over thee and to instruct thee, and to guide thee every hour. Oh, beloved, would you realize what that is, "Having boldness to enter into the Holiest of all"? Believe that you have a High Priest over the house of God, a Minister of the Sanctuary, into whose keeping God will give you. "Let us draw nigh." We can do so with Jesus, the living Jesus, to bring us in.

Another work of the Priest is to communicate to us all the blessings that we are to receive as we tarry in the Holiest of all. What is it that I am to do when I am in the Holiest? I am there to learn what worship is. To learn what it is to sink down into ever-deepening humility before God. There it is that I am to be clothed upon with the likeness and the spirit and the beauty of Jesus. There it is that I am to receive afresh, every day, the outflow and the inflow of the Holy Spirit from my beloved Head.

How can I attain to these things? Beloved fellow believers, you have a living High Priest who waits every moment to do His perfect work in you. All that you long for as you tarry in the Holy Place, you may count upon Jesus, the High Priest, to do for you in power. Let us take to heart this one work of Christ. "He died, the just for the unjust, that he might bring us unto God"; or as in Hebrews 7, "A better hope whereby we draw nigh to God."

To bring us nearer to God is the great object of the priesthood of Jesus. You know practically just as much, or as little, of the priesthood of Jesus as you have much, or have little, of the nearness of God. Is it what your heart longs for? "Nearer, my God, to Thee." How often we have sung it! Oh! take today, with large faith, the blessed truth again of the work of the High Priest, the God-man Jesus. It is to bring and to keep me near to my God. I can count upon Him to do it. Will you count upon Him for that? Let every heart say, "Amen, I will trust Jesus to keep me near to God." And then, whatever desires you have, whatever needs you feel, whatever hopes arise in you, depend upon the fact that Christ will and Christ can fulfill them all.

That is the meaning of the word, He is the "Minister of the Sanctuary"—the Minister of that heavenly place into which we are to go and where we are to live. But now comes the great difficulty. "Alas, my sinful heart! How can I ever hope to live all day in the presence of my God, in the Holiest of all! Here is my feeble nature, here is my faithless heart, and here, too, are my circumstances, so trying and full of temptation. For hours and hours I am often compelled to concentrate all the attention of my mind and heart on some worldly business. I do it in the Lord's name, and yet my heart is occupied with these things." Listen, brother, while I tell you of the other name of Jesus: He is the "Mediator of the New Covenant."

What does that mean? He is not only, as we heard a little while ago, the surety of the Covenant. Even that word "surety" means more than we think. At the beginning He was my surety when He paid the debt; but that was only the beginning. Christ is my surety that the Covenant will be fulfilled in me. He is my surety for what I need today. And oh! He is that surety because He is the "Mediator of the New Covenant."

You know what that New Covenant is? You have read the beautiful account we have of it, from Jeremiah, in Hebrews 8: "Their sins and iniquities will I remember no more." That is the first; but there is a second: "I will put my laws into their mind, and write them in their hearts."

Then there is the third: "They shall not teach every man his neighbour, and every man his brother, saying, Know the Lord: for all shall know me, from the least to the greatest."

Now, it is the work of our High Priest to see that that Covenant is fulfilled. He has to mediate, to pass down from heaven, to secure and make actual in my heart every moment the reality of giving me something far more than just the thought that I have been pardoned, and that every time I fail I can get pardon again. Christ can, by His Spirit, lead us into the wonderful power of His blood, so that we may know what it is to have a constant trust in Him and to have no more remembrance of the sin that has been put away. Christ Jesus is able to make the power of His blood such a reality that the life of God can shine unbrokenly in my poor heart.

In chapter 9, just where we read of Christ's entering the tabernacle and the Holiest with His blood, there follows immediately in regard to the human side, "How much more shall the blood of Christ cleanse your conscience from all dead works, to serve the living God?" Oh, have you such an apprehension of what Christ's blood can do? Do you long for it? There is no word that fills me more with wonder and admiration than that precious word, "the blood of Christ." Oh, let us know that blood which our High Priest applies. Let our souls rejoice in Him. Let us ask Jesus to keep us in the full enjoyment of this, the first blessing of the Covenant.

Then comes the second blessing, "I will write my law in their hearts." Praise God! What does it mean to have a law in the heart? It means this: To have the knowledge and the will and the power of God's law inspired into us. For example, when I speak of an acorn, how do I know that it will grow up into a mighty oak tree that may stand for a hundred years? Because the law of the oak tree has been written in the heart of the acorn. The acorn may be small, and the oak tree may be spreading its branches for a hundred years to come, but it was all in the acorn. Even so with Christ, the Mediator of the Covenant, the one on whom I can depend to make the Covenant true. Christ, my High Priest, is to see that the Spirit of the Lord God shall be and live in me, rule in me, conquer in me, and work out all His blessed purposes in me. Christ, the High Priest, is Mediator of the Covenant for this blessing too —a life that lives out the law written in the heart.

And now let us consider the last blessing— immediate and unbroken fellowship with God. The prophet leads us on into the fullness of the blessing: "A man shall not need to say any more to his brother, Know the Lord," for there will be direct, immediate, personal communication between God and the soul. "All shall know him, from the least even to the greatest." Beloved, Christ is the Mediator of the Covenant. He is not only Minister of the Sanctuary in heaven, but also the Mediator of the Covenant on earth.

Just think, for a moment, why these two

things must go together. That will make clear to us the blessedness of this priestly work. We know that every creature is constituted according to the kingdom to which it belongs. A plant belongs to the vegetable kingdom, an animal belongs to the animal kingdom, and each must have a constitution according to the nature of that kingdom. Take an ox. Why is it that you can nowhere make an ox so happy as in a field of rich grass? A lion would not be at home there to find its food, nor would a man. But the ox nature and the grass are suited to each other.

Why is it that some people, when brought into rich homes, are made unhappy? Because their nature is accustomed to wretchedness and poverty. And why is it that Jesus said to Nicodemus, "Except a man be born again, he cannot enter the kingdom of God"? It was for the same reason. I must have a nature in harmony with the Kingdom.

And now, what good is it that Christ is the Minister of the Sanctuary, that the most wonderful promises are open to me, and that I may enter into the Holiest of all, if I have not the power, the sympathy, the heart that is prepared to dwell there? Alas! sometimes Christians have read those promises almost with despair. They have said, "It is not for me; my heart is not fit for it." But let me tell you, Jesus Christ taught us to pray, "As in heaven, so upon earth," and He works it himself. As Minister of the Sanctuary, He keeps heaven open for you every moment; as Mediator of the Covenant, He is fitting you every moment for it. If you will trust Him and His blood to cleanse you, He is willing to breathe the law of God within you, and himself to be the bond of fellowship with God. May Christ make the covenant a reality in your life.

I fear we too often look at Jesus as an outward Saviour. We think of Aaron and what he did with the blood of bulls and of goats, and then we multiply that by millions and millions and say there is no comparison. Christ's blood is divinely precious, and Christ himself is the divine Saviour; but still we do very little else than just magnify the work of Aaron into immensity or infinity. We do not know what the absolute difference is; but the work of Aaron was an outward work, and the work of Christ is an inward work.

The sun is many hundreds of thousands of miles away from us, but on a cold day you go out and say, "I am going into the sun." And the sun actually comes into you and passes through your marrow and blood, warming that which was benumbed and ready to freeze and die. Just so, my Lord Jesus is in inconceivable glory. But, oh, by His divine grace, He is the Mediator of the Covenant, and I can come not only into His presence as He is in heaven, but the light and warmth of His love can shine into me, even here upon earth! He is fitting me, as a poor, sinful child of the world, to walk with God, to enjoy real and true fellowship with God, to dwell in the love of God, and to follow Him.

Oh, friends, we do not understand the words we use when we speak of these things! They are

31

too high and too wonderful. But, still, let us use them all the same, and let us pray to God to make His wonderful redeeming love our full and daily experience. Let Jesus be our High Priest—the Minister of the Sanctuary, opening heaven to our hearts; the Mediator of the Covenant, opening our hearts for heaven to enter in and fill them.

What is all this to end in? What is the object of all this? Is it that I am to live in God's presence that I may be very happy and very holy? Verily no. These things are but the means to an end. What is it then? It is that I, like Christ, should also be a priest.

You all know that wonderful thought connected with Aaron. God made Aaron high priest in such a sense that his life carried priesthood to all his descendants. Through fifteen hundred years a descendant of Aaron was priest, because he was a son of Aaron. The life of Aaron carried the blessing. And, oh, the life, the divine life, of my High Priest! Do you think that that would carry less blessing than the priesthood of Aaron? Verily no.

Time will not allow me to allude to the deep meaning of the priesthood of Melchizedek—one that never dies, but lives in the power of an eternal life, working every moment. We have that precious word in Hebrews 7: "He was made a priest after the power of an endless life." Yes, Jesus Christ imparts His own life to us. I have referred already to what we see in Exodus—the priesthood, the means of the indwelling. In Hebrews 5 it is said that Christ did not exalt himself to be High Priest, but God said unto Him, "My Son, this day have I begotten thee."

The priesthood of Christ! Is that a dead doctrine? No, indeed. The priesthood has its root in the sonship. The divine life of the Son is what gives the priesthood its power to bring us nigh to God—to bring us into His life, and His life into us. It means that all the love and holiness of God dwells in the Son. The sonship means that when He takes us up and we are made partakers with Christ, we not only get a pardon that is outside but we get the Holy Ghost within us. Jesus, the High Priest, does His work within us. He gives us His own life. We cannot have the benefit of the priesthood in full power except as the power of regeneration works and Jesus comes as the indwelling One to reveal himself. If we begin to understand that, then we shall see what is meant by the fact that we are called, all of us, to be priests, because we have the very life of the High Priest in us—not only imputed, but the High Priest dwelling within us.

And that brings us to the concluding thought. Believers, I ask you all, why are we considering the priesthood of Jesus? Is it only that we can know better how our sins can be blotted out and conquered? Is it only because we want to know better how we can enter into the Holiest and dwell there in the full light of God's love? If so, there is a basic misunderstanding of the priesthood.

What does priesthood mean? Self-sacrifice to

the death for God and for man. That was the spirit of Jesus, and that is the spirit that Jesus wants to breathe into every priestly heart that is willing to yield itself to Him. Oh, brother, He, through the eternal Spirit, gave himself up to God, a sacrifice without a spot. And when I receive of that eternal Spirit into me, the priesthood of Jesus becomes a reality and the double work that Jesus does becomes my work too. Praise God! it becomes your work. And what is that work, that double work? You go even into the Holiest of all as an intercessor.

What could I not say upon this blessed subject if I had time—the need there is for Christians getting more definite training from Christ in the work of intercession? Let me say a word to all who have the command of their own time. Have you ever thought that in heaven Jesus has the command of His own time, and He spends it in unceasing intercession? "He ever liveth to make intercession for us." Have you ever thought of the glory that this gives to prayer?

If this day you claim afresh the priesthood of Christ as your only hope, then pray for the spirit of intercession. By the grace of God, begin to pray more for the perishing world around you, pray for Christ's feeble, sickly Church, pray for God's servants in Christendom and in heathendom. Live in this faith: "I have become united to the High Priest, and He has given me a priestly heart that intercession might be made not only at times but continually from me and from every member of the Body."

34

I said that with the priest in Israel there were two thoughts: "he shall stand before my face to minister" and "he shall go out to bless the people." That is what Christ does: He intercedes above, and He sends the blessing down. And that is the double work every priest has to <u>do</u>: to ask and bring down the blessing from above, and then to go out and dispense it. I know it is the prayer of many an earnest heart, "God, help us that this may not be a time of spiritual self-indulgence. God, help us that we may not be feeding upon old or upon new truth while our hearts do not beat for our fellow creatures."

We have spoken about the High Priest who gave up His place upon the throne and came to this earth to give His life and His blood. There is a place for you on earth with Him and in Him. Give yourself up to follow Jesus, even to Calvary.

"O my High Priest, breathe Thy Spirit into me! Breathe Thy priestly Spirit into me! I am a member of Thy Body; I have Thy life in me. Like Thee, I am a priest. I am Thine! Holy Jesus, breathe Thy Spirit into me and let me only and ever be with Thee that Thou mayest be glorified and my fellowmen blessed." God will make the blessing ours.

CHAPTER THREE

THE LORD JESUS CHRIST:
Our Way into the Holiest

"Oh, the blessedness of a life in the Holiest! Here the Father is seen and His love tasted. Here His holiness is revealed and the soul made partaker of it. Here the sacrifice of love and worship and adoration, the incense of prayer and supplication, is offered in power. Here the outpouring of the Spirit is known as an everstreaming, overflowing river, from under the throne of God and the Lamb. Here the soul, in God's presence, grows into more complete oneness with Christ, and more entire conformity to His likeness. Here, in union with Christ, in His unceasing intercession, we are emboldened to take our place as intercessors who can have power with God and prevail. Here the soul mounts up as on eagles' wings, the strength is renewed, and the blessing and the power and the love are imparted with which God's priests can go out to bless a dying world. Here each day we may experience the fresh anointing, in virtue of which we can go out to be the bearers, the witnesses, and channels of God's salvation to men, and living instruments through whom our blessed King works out His full and final triumph. 'O Jesus, our great High Priest, let this be our life!' "
—*The Holiest of All*

In Hebrews 10: 19 you find these words, "having therefore." With this verse the second half of the epistle begins, and that "therefore" sums up the whole previous nine chapters. "Having therefore, brethren, boldness to enter into the holiest by the blood of Jesus, by a new and living way, which he hath consecrated for us, through the veil, that is to say, his flesh; and having an High Priest over the house of God; let us draw near." That is the one lesson of the epistle as of the whole of Holy Scripture—"let us draw near." The work of the priesthood is to bring us near to God. "Let us draw near with a true heart in full assurance of faith, having our hearts sprinkled from an evil conscience, and our bodies washed with pure water. Let us hold fast the profession of our faith without wavering; (for he is faithful that promised;) and let us consider one another to provoke unto love and to good works: not forsaking the assembling of ourselves together, as the manner of some is; but exhorting one another; and so much the more, as ye see the day approaching."

The words from which I wish to speak are in the 19th to the first half of the 22nd verse, and especially these words, "Let us draw near."

That is not addressed to the unconverted. It does not speak of conversion. It includes that, but it is spoken to Christians, to the Hebrew Christians. It is said to believers: "Let us draw near." It supposes that there are believers (and the Hebrews were among them) who did not live as near to God as they might. They had wandered, they had not been diligent in pressing on to the fullness of gospel truth, and they were not living in the nearness of God. A child can be a dear child and yet be far away from the father. "Let us draw near." The message is very specially to believers.

Then, it does not mean, let us draw near in prayer. It is often so understood and, indeed, is applicable to prayer; but it means far more. I cannot be praying the whole day, in the sense of speaking to God. I have my business to attend to, and God wants that I should do so, and be just as near to Him there as when I pray. "Let us draw near." It is meant to cover the whole life—every day and every moment. It is not a nearness of thought. I can think, and imagine, and argue that Christ's blood is shed, that there is access for me, and that I have the right of coming nigh; and yet I may be only thinking and arguing about the nearness without living and enjoying it. No, it means really, actually, experimentally, spiritually: let us draw near to God. It does not mean, let us draw near sometimes. It means, as with a child who has wandered from his father, let us draw near and abide near. Nearness to God is the great blessing of our High Priest; let us take it and use it. We read in Ephesians, "We have been brought nigh by the blood of Christ." Let us live in that nearness to God.

And now, if we want to obey this command, we ought to set before us very distinctly what our life ought to be. We have access into the Holiest. The Holiest is now to be our home. Just a word about that. God wants us to live every day and all the day in His holy presence. Where God is, there it is heaven. The presence of God means heaven; and God is omnipresent. We all believe that. And the difference between an unconverted man and the believer is this: the unconverted man does not recognize the presence of God, while the converted man often thinks of it and desires after it—too often, however, only as a thing for times and seasons. But the man who goes on to perfection, according to the teaching of the epistle, accepts and claims the abiding presence of his God as his continuing, unchanging experience.

Dear friends, are there any hearts longing for that—without interruption, without a break, to abide in God's presence? You tell me, "That is impossible. My business, my duties prevent it." No, I want to make you understand that the presence of God is something He will take care of. He will take care that you shall have it, whether you keep thinking of Him or not. Look at the sun, and look at the people in the street. Have you seen any of them taking the trouble to secure the shining of the sun? No, the sun shines without their concern or mine. God takes care that the sun shines; the sun takes care that there is always light flooding us. We only have to come out into the light and enjoy it. And God! Will He not take care that His light always shines upon us? If we fully believe that, I think one great difficulty will be out of the way.

People always think, "What can I do?" and,

"Shall I really be able to live thus?" My brothers and sisters, come today and think of what God can do. God can do wonders. We have just to draw near and trust and give up ourselves to lead this blessed life. When we wait upon and trust Jesus, the great High Priest, He will make it a reality.

You complain of your feebleness against sin. I want to lead you to a place today where God will enable you to conquer sin. This place is the Holiest of all, His presence. You complain of your feebleness in work. I want to lead you to a place where God will breathe His Spirit upon you every day and give you new strength for work. You complain of so many difficulties and troubles. The Father hath prepared for you a home, a resting place, in His own home, in His very presence. Do you believe it? Do believe it! And Jesus is the doorkeeper, the Minister of the Sanctuary, the Priest in the Temple, who will bring you in and teach you how to have the love always to be pleasing to God.

Now, let us look at the four great arguments found in the verses preceding the command, "Let us draw near"—the four great arguments to encourage us to draw near. First, "having boldness to enter the holiest." The Holiest is opened up. Second, "having boldness by the blood." The blood gives you the boldness. Third, "having a new and living way." The way will carry you. Fourth, "having a High Priest over the house of God." The High Priest will watch over you. Let us draw near.

First of all, the Holiest has been opened up, "having boldness to enter the holiest." You know from your Bibles what the Holiest was in the tabernacle. The tabernacle consisted of two rooms or compartments. One (we may call it the front one) was where the priests lived and served. They were allowed to walk in and out continually in the service of God. The other room (the hinder compartment) was separated from the front one by a thick veil. There God dwelt, between the cherubims on the Ark of the Covenant in a cloud, and no man was allowed to enter through that veil or look behind it on pain of death.

Just think what an extraordinary thing this is. God has said, "I want to come to my people, to dwell among them, and I want to let them dwell with me." But He went (I say it with reverence) and shut himself up in a dark place, and none of them could come to see their God or meet Him. Only the high priest might, once a year for a few minutes, enter in. But he had to go out again, at once; and if he or any priest entered in, immediate death was the punishment. God had His abode, but written over that abode were these words: "No admission on pain of death." For fifteen hundred years God kept the people away from direct contact with himself.

But what happened? All at once, one day, the veil of the temple was rent in twain from top to bottom; and the amazed priests, who were in the holy place, saw the Holiest of all opened up. They rushed out with terror and fear lest they

41

should die. How did that come? At that moment Christ was dying. His death and His blood rent the veil and gave access into God's presence. What does that mean? Does it mean only that Christ should, fifty days after His death, ascend to heaven and enter within the veil? Thank God it means that. But there is a great deal more. It means that you and I are called to enter inside the veil. When? Not at death, but now—now, by union with our living High Priest, by faith in the love of God that has welcomed us to Him.

Brother, if you had been a priest in Israel, would not your heart sometimes have longed, "Oh that I had the privilege of the high priest to go into God's very presence!" And yet you would have thought, "It is only for a moment; even the high priest has to come out again." There hung that veil, God's great object lesson, for fifteen hundred years. Man must not come too near God. The Israelites could come into the outer court, and the priests into the holy place, but no one may come too near God.

The veil is now rent, and the command comes to you to come into the most complete and intimate nearness. God wants His children, by the Holy Spirit, to draw very near, to enter and to dwell in His very presence. I pray you, do believe God means it. It is the place prepared for us.

When a son comes from a long journey, having been absent for years, with what loving care the mother prepares a room for him. And when he comes, the mother says, "Here is your room; see, we have made it nice for you. You must come and stay here now." Today God comes and says, "My children, I have prepared the best room for you. The place where I dwell, there you must dwell."

The place where Jesus entered with His blood, there you can enter. You must enter! He says, "I want you to enter in and dwell in my love." Oh, come, let us draw near. If there are any whose hearts tell them, "Alas! I have not been living in this union. I am no nearer to God now than in the days of my first conversion. I have known what it was to believe, but into this abiding union, into this daily experience of the presence of God resting upon me from morning till night, I have not entered"—to you comes the message: "Let us draw near." What will be your answer? "Blessed Father, I come; take me in."

Secondly, "having boldness by the blood." I know what the great difficulty is that troubles you. There is the thought running through many a heart, "Oh sin, sin, sin! With a sinful nature it is impossible always to be dwelling in the Holiest of all." Listen now! "Having boldness to enter in by the blood"—would that God might reveal to us what that means! Oh, I am afraid you do not give the blood of Jesus the honor that God means you to give it. God honors that blood as infinitely, inconceivably precious. It is to Him worth more than anyone can tell—the obedience of His beloved Son! Oh! that we would take the trouble to find out, "What is that blood worth to me?"

In Israel, what honor they gave to the blood of a lamb or a heifer! In connection with Christ's blood, we read in Hebrews of cleansing by the ashes of a heifer. A heifer was sacrificed and the blood of that sacrifice sprinkled before the tabernacle of the congregation. The heifer was then burned with other items and the ashes kept for purification. When a person touched a dead body, he was unclean. The prepared ashes were then mixed with pure water and sprinkled upon the person. What happened then?

Up to the time that he was sprinkled, he was kept out of the fellowship of God's people, and out of the court; but when he had been sprinkled he was clean. He then proved his trust in the blood of the heifer by boldly coming back and taking his place as a cleansed and restored man. He was restored to his people and to the presence of God.

The blood of the sacrifice was of such value to the unclean person that even the ashes of the sacrifice were considered sufficient for cleansing. If the blood and the ashes of the heifer were considered cleansing agents, I ask, what honor then ought we not give to the blood of the Son of God?

You tell me, "I cannot understand all that the Bible teaches about the cleansing of the blood. I hear differences in expressions used. Tell me, what does it mean?" God forbid that

44

you should wait for this! Do not seek to find your rest in different expressions of belief, or in having your own correct theory. But, I pray you, if you have any difficulty at all, come at once. There is something far beyond understanding, and that is faith. Honor the precious blood by believing that the blood can bring you nigh and the blood can keep you nigh. Say today, "However sinful I feel myself, that is not going to keep me back from trusting God! The blood— the blood of Jesus—is my boldness and my confidence."

"Having boldness by the blood"—I want you, for a moment, to try and realize what that means. What is the worth and the power of that blood? When Christ approached heaven as the Mediator and Surety of guilty man, and when He asked entrance into heaven not only for himself but for all mankind who should believe in Him, what, think you, was the answer given at the gate of heaven? If there had been an angel doorkeeper to ask, "How canst thou demand access for all that race of guilty men?" the answer of Jesus would have been, "My blood is their ransom! I have conquered sin. I have made an end of it and put it away. I have satisfied the Father. I have access to the Father." And, oh, if Christ went in thus in our name, shall we not honor the blood? Shall we not trust the blood? Shall we not say in the midst of all difficulties, "I cannot understand or explain all, but I can trust the infinite power of the blood of the Lamb. This is my boldness!"

Oh, beloved, believe in that blood today; honor it, even now, by boldly claiming your place in the nearness of God. That blood is able not only to bring you in now and again, but it is the blood of a sacrifice, shed once for all and forever. And in that everlasting power, it can keep you ever abiding in God's presence. Ask Jesus, by the power of His Holy Spirit, to make the cleansing of your heart with that precious blood a living reality, truth, and life; and the blood will be your boldness every moment. It will give you confidence to say: "I can dwell with God all the day. As long as the blood speaks for me, I may confidently claim the everlasting and ever-abiding nearness."

Then comes the third argument, "having a new and living way." Not only is the Holiest opened up and we are given boldness through the blood, but there is also "a new and living way." What is that? It is the way that Christ opened up "through the veil, that is, through his flesh." In other words, it is the way of the cross, the way of death.

In death on the cross, God condemned sin in the flesh. The flesh was the veil that separated Christ from God. He had dwelt with God, but He came outside the veil and lived a life of trial, temptation, prayer, struggle, and faith. His flesh was, in a very real sense, the veil between God and man. But Christ rent that veil by giving His flesh to be rent and broken on Calvary. This is the way of the rent veil. The flesh given up to the will of God, even to death, is the new way He opened up.

In the beginning of Hebrews 10 you will find that the old way was "by sacrifices," the sacrifices of animals; but Christ came, and in doing the will of God He opened a new and living way. And now, dear Christians, here comes the most difficult part. There are many Christians who long to enter into the presence of God, but they do not want to come by the new and living way. They think a great deal about the blood and the title and right it gives them to enter in, but they do not understand this way by which we must walk. Christ is the Way. That means, in the way in which He lived I must live; in the way in which He walked I must walk.

Are you willing to draw near to God in the way in which Christ drew near to Him? Understand, the nearness of God is not a thing of locality; it is a thing of disposition and will—it is a spiritual thing. I may be sitting next to a man, and yet in heart and inclination I may be at the greatest distance from him and might abhor what he thinks about. Another man may be far away from me, say in South Africa, and yet I may be in the most intimate nearness with him in love, in similarity of disposition and purpose. And so the nearness of God is a nearness of life, a nearness of sympathy, a nearness of love.

Oh, brother, here is the new and living way by which I have come: giving up my will in obedience unto death. The blood has set the door wide open, but there is a way in which we must walk. Christ is my living path and my living leader, and it is as I give up my will and my life in self-sacrifice, like Christ, that I draw near to God.

O Christian! I am afraid there is a great deal of comfortable Christianity that wants to be converted, and to be saved, and to be made happy; but it is not the Christianity of Christ. The Christianity of Christ means that you must give up everything to God. It means that you must give up your whole will to God. It means that you must give your life a sacrifice to God every hour of the day. Christ's call is: "Let a man deny himself, and take up his cross, and follow me."

There are Christians who do not want to walk in that path of self-denial. I dare not say how a man ought to sacrifice himself; but I dare say this, that every true believer will be asking God sometimes and often, "O my God, what wouldest Thou have me sacrifice more for Thy sake?" Remember that prayer. Walk in the path of Jesus. Pray often, "Lord, teach Thy people, and teach me to know what the new way is that Christ opened—the way of death unto life, the way of obedience into glory, the way of humiliation into the highest exaltation."

You say, "This is a hard saying. All that you told us about the Holiest of all opened up was beautiful; and all you said about the blood was precious; but now it comes too hard upon us. We are weak, and we can't walk the way of Christ."

Listen now to what the Word says to meet your difficulty. The new way is a *living way*. What does that mean? All our paths and streets are dead ways. If I have not the strength to walk along the street, the street won't carry me. If the car or tram or bus has not some power to move itself, the street won't move it. These ways are all dead.

But, praise God, there is one living way. It is this: When a poor, helpless sinner, who cannot move a foot, casts himself upon Jesus to become conformable to Him; gives up his heart and will to walk in the self-sacrifice of Jesus; then the Way takes him up and lifts him on. What is that living way? It is the power of the Holy Spirit of Jesus.

Listen, Jesus did not walk in that way, go to heaven and leave me behind in my own strength to walk like Him. Never! Jesus went to heaven and then sent down the Holy Spirit by whom He had walked in that new way. And that Holy Spirit will strengthen me, so that in Christ, who is the Way, I walk even as He walked. The way is a difficult one, a hard one, a way of submission and humiliation and death. But, thank God, it is a living way if we but once surrender ourselves to it. The Spirit of God will be our strength and our joy.

And then, lastly, "and having an High Priest over the house of God." We have had three great lessons, three great motives, for drawing near; but the fourth is the best of all. I have had the Holiest of all set open; I have had the blood given me as my assurance every hour and every moment; I have had the new way set before me as a living way, that from hour to hour will carry me. But yet I have not all I want. The last is the best—the living person of my living Lord Jesus Christ.

"Having an High Priest"—just think of that word "having." We have "such an High Priest." How have I? In thought? He is in heaven, and I have Him here? Ah, no! I have a house in South Africa, but I have no enjoyment of it today, for I am here in England. And many people have Jesus as their Saviour in heaven, but so little do they enjoy Him. But here, praise God, we have the liberty to say we have a High Priest in personal enjoyment. How can that be? I can have Jesus in no other way than in my heart. I cannot have Him with my hands, my mouth, my eyes. My thoughts have not a spiritual and divine object. My thoughts can think about it, but they cannot have it. But the heart! Oh, that I could tell every believer, "With your heart you have Him." Occupy yourself more with this blessed truth, and believe it out to the very end. I have the Almighty God, the great Priest, the living, sympathizing Jesus, over the house of God. I have Him—not a bit of Him, not something of Him, but the whole undivided Almighty Jesus. I have Him, praise God.

Oh, souls, take time to believe this. Take time to worship until your heart is filled. I have a great High Priest to watch over this wonderful life in the sanctuary. I have Jesus; and when sin comes, He makes everything right up above as well as here below and within. I have Jesus, and He leads me along that new and living way. I have Jesus within my heart. I have Him and hold Him. I love Him and trust Him. Jesus Christ does indeed bring me into the presence of God. When it cost Him the agony of Gethsemane and the death on Calvary, He did not refuse; but He went to the very uttermost that He might open it up to me.

And now that the price is paid, the blood shed, the door opened, and the heart of the Father made glad, will my Lord Jesus refuse to take me in? God forbid that such a thought should enter our hearts! Jesus lives to take us in and to keep us in.

Now, what is to be the fruit of our meditation upon the priesthood of Jesus? Is it to be this, that from today you will live nearer to God, more full of the joy of His presence? Is it that from today you will honor the blood as you have never honored it before, to bring you deeper into the inner sanctuary? Is it that from today you will give up yourself to the new and living way, the way of self-sacrifice in the power of the Holy Ghost? Is it that you will learn to trust Jesus and give yourself entirely to Him that He may do His work in you and bring you nigh to God? Oh, beloved, the High Priest does this work by dwelling in the heart. Come, let us now open our hearts wide to Him. Oh, come, and as we have gazed upon His work—from Calvary to the throne in glory, and from the throne back again into our hearts, and from our hearts back again to the presence of God into which He brings us—let every heart say, "Jesus, I have Thee! I have Thee!"

Beloved Christians, accept Him now with a new acceptance. Take hold of Him now with a new hold. "Jesus, Minister of the Sanctuary, High Priest, and King, I have Thee, I have Thee! And Thou hast me, Lord, and we part not forever. I am linked to Thee by the power of Thy blood!" And having Jesus as our High Priest, let us draw near, let us draw near, let us draw near!

"The joy of our Lord's inner life was in love, in the love which always pleased the Father, which always obeyed His will, which always lived in His presence. And just in proportion as we have fellowship with Him in this—for He puts before us no lower standard, but calls us into the same relationship with himself as He had with the Father—shall we have fellowship in His joy. When the soul is brought into conformity with Jesus, there is the sunshine of God's smile without a cloud between. The law of holiness is the law of joy."—Mrs. Pennefather

CHAPTER FOUR

THE LORD JESUS CHRIST:
The Food of the Soul

"This blessed table is 'the Lord's Table.' It is not the table of any particular church or congregation; it is the banquet which the Lord of glory provides for His subjects, which the Father of mercies spreads for His sons and daughters, to which the Redeemer bids His disciples, that their love may be rekindled, and their faith increased; and where the Holy Ghost reveals to the faithful the treasures which are hid in Emmanuel! In rightly partaking of this banquet we look back to the 'full, perfect, and sufficient sacrifice' made for sinners, when our Saviour Jesus Christ cried on the cross: 'It is finished.' We look up, and by faith behold the living Redeemer, who sustains the life that He hath given; and we look onward to that glorious hour when the marriage of the Lamb shall be consummated, and His blood-bought bride shall sit down at the heavenly feast, amidst the anthems of unnumbered angels and in the radiance of her Father's presence. 'Blessed are they that are called to the marriage supper of the Lamb.' "—Rev. W. Pennefather

"The cup of blessing, which we bless, is it not the communion of the blood of Christ? [In the margin of the Revised Version we read, 'the participation.'] The bread which we break, is it not the communion of the body of Christ? for we, being many, are one bread and one body, for we are all partakers of that one bread" (I Cor. 10: 16, 17).

Life and food are dependent upon each other. The nature of the life decides the character of the food. The lion eats flesh, and the ox eats grass, each according to its nature. On the other hand, the character of the food will decide the growth, and the strength, and the increase of the life. You know that in food there are very different elements of nourishment. A medical man will give to one what will strengthen the bones, if they be weak; he has another sort of food for the person who needs muscle. The food will decide the character and the strength of the life.

What is the food we need for our immortal spirits? We need the body and the blood of the Son of God. Oh, mystery of mysteries, that Jesus says, "I came from heaven to give my flesh to be the life of the world!" Surely it is of consequence that we understand aright what this means. I must not only look upon Christ as the bread of my life, but especially upon the broken body and the shed blood—upon the dying Christ. The death of Christ must be my chief nourishment.

Let us look at this. You know that the death of Christ is His chief characteristic. He came from heaven with a commandment from the Father, that He should lay down His life. Christ lived His whole life in the spirit of preparation, offering himself for death as the consummation of His work. He died! Without that He never could have risen again, nor have ascended the throne. In heaven He still reminds us, "I am he that liveth and was dead, and I am alive for evermore." Through eternity, He is on the throne as the Lamb that was slain, and the saints never cease singing of the preciousness of His blood. "Thou hast purchased us unto God by thy blood!" Brother, the chief glory of Christ is His death.

If I am to feed upon Christ, I must specially feed upon His death. What does that mean? Look at it a moment. For instance, plants, trees, and flowers have a certain food prepared and put into the soil for them. Take something so simple as bone fertilizer; in the bone you have an external substance into which the plant inserts its rootlets, passing through all the little cells of the bone and taking out from it its very life-essence. It does not take up a single grain of the substance itself, but it takes the very essence of what is in the bone. This it works up into the sap; and then the spirit that is in the plant, received from the food in the soil, creates the leaves and the flowers and the fruit in their beauty. Just so too, in our bodies, we take what the medical man prescribes to meet the weakness in our constitution—some preparation with different elements in it, but we take it all in one. There it is, in some shape, bodily, but it disappears; it enters our blood; its life elements enter into and become one with our life and strengthen our frame.

How can I feed on the death of Christ? Feeding upon a thing means taking its inmost essence into your being. When I feed on meat, or on bread, or on anything else, I take its life-power into my constitution. And what does it now mean, feeding upon the body and blood of Jesus? Let me give you a few thoughts, very simple and short. I must find out what the death of Christ signifies and what its inmost spirit is. By faith, I must then accept it, and appropriate it, and look up to Jesus to work it within me in His divine power.

Now, what does the death of Christ mean? First, what does it mean in its *relation to sin?* It means this, that Christ counted sin an accursed thing; and He was willing to give His life to get our life out from under the curse of sin. When I feed upon the death of Christ, it means that I count sin an accursed thing; that I acknowledge that sin has power over the whole of my natural life; that I consent to say, "I want to die away from sin." There is no separation from sin but by death; and I want the power of Christ's death to work in me that I may be made free from sin. That is what the apostle teaches us in Romans 6.

Have you ever noticed how both baptism and the Lord's Supper have to do with nothing but the death of Christ? Now, how can I live so that I do not continue in sin? Just know that you are baptized into the death of Christ, and then feed upon His death. That means that I accept the terrible curse of all sin. I accept the proof that all my life is under the power of sin, and that there is no way of getting rid of it but by the absolute death in Christ.

Next, what did Christ's death mean in *relation to the world?* It meant this: Christ and the world met each other; and in the temptation in the wilderness, the Prince of the world tried to effect a compromise, a reconciliation between Christ and the world. Christ was not, however, of the world, and He would not have a kingdom of this world. The controversy was settled on Calvary. There Christ allowed the world to crucify Him, to prove that it was an irreconcilable enmity to Him. Christ's death meant this: The world hates me because I am not of it; I am crucified to the world and the world to me.

And now, if I feed upon the death of Jesus Christ—the broken body and the shed blood—this means that I want to take this element of the crucifixion up into my spiritual life. This element is separation from the world, antagonism to the world; it means to be crucified to the world and to have the world crucified to me. That was what made Paul glory in the Cross. It was not only atonement and it was not only pardon, glorious as these gifts are, but it was the fellowship of the Cross he gloried in.

Oh! dear friends, let us long for it. The world that we live in is the world that rejected Christ; it will have nothing to do with the rule of Christ as King. Let us follow Christ and go out of the camp. And as we feed upon His body and blood, let this be our prayer, "Oh, my Father, may the Spirit which was in Christ when He died on the

Cross—separation from the world—may the spirit of Christ's death dwell with me." As I said before, of that on which I feed I take out its life elements and absorb them into my constitution. That is what I do in my participation of the body and blood of Christ in its separation from the world. I want the death of Christ to be the ruling power of my whole being.

Look at the death of Christ again in its *relation to God*. What was it? It was the giving up of His own will to the will of the Father forever. It was unparalleled humility that made Him say, "I am nothing, and God is all." It was that which made Him willing to die. It was the declaration, "My will as compared with the will of God shall never be of any value. I give up my will, I give up mysef to be nothing; God must be all." That was the spirit of Christ's death. And when I say, "O Jesus, feed me with Thy broken body and with Thy shed blood," it means nothing less than to say, "Let the dispositions and the inclinations and the tempers which urged Thee on to Calvary— let them dwell in me, my Lord. I want to feed upon Thy death; let that become the nutriment and the characteristic of my life."

Beloved, are you perhaps struggling against the outbreaks of your own will and your pride? Are you still at times self-willed, battling with God? Are you seeking exaltation in any shape? I pray you today, come feed upon the broken body and the shed blood of the Lamb of God, who in meekness and lowliness of heart, humbled himself and became obedient unto death.

Humility, obedience to God, surrender to God's will—this is the secret of Gethsemane and of Calvary.

"O Jesus, feed us today! Feed us with the heavenly bread, the body and the blood which are the proof and the power of Thy most blessed and complete surrender to the will of God, of Thy divine and most perfect humility."

Once more, what is the death of Christ in its *relation to men?* It is a death for men. Yes, you cannot partake of the death of Christ without remembering His dying love to lost sinners. What moved Him to come to die? He did not need it for himself. He did not need to bear the curse, and to be crucified to the world, and to give up His will to the Father. The inspiration of it all was love to men. And if I am going to feed upon a crucified Christ, I must be prepared, I must be hungry, I must have a heart that longs to have this element of the heavenly food enter my being. I must be ready to give up myself, like Jesus, to live and die for my fellowmen. I am not come here to eat food for my mere enjoyment. Verily, no: food from heaven to strengthen me for heaven's work; food from Calvary to strengthen me for Calvary's work; the crucified Christ that I may be fitted to carry the crucified Christ in my life to my fellowmen.

Brethren, you all know how Paul reminds us that we are "to shew forth the Lord's death until he come." How am I to do that? By thinking of it, and speaking of it, and trusting in it, and eating and drinking in commemoration? Yes, but that is not all. I am to show the death of the Lord in my body, in my life. That is showing forth the death of the Lord. You know those words of Paul so well, "carrying about the dying of the Lord Jesus in the body, that the life of Jesus may be made manifest." How can you make manifest the life of Christ? By having the death of Christ working in you. You know that when Paul had been more than twenty years an apostle, as an aged man he still cried, "I count all things but loss, if I may know him . . . in the fellowship of his sufferings, being made conformable to his death."

We spoke before about the new and living way. Is not that it? You long, like Jesus, to die for your fellowmen. Come, eat this bread and drink this wine that the power of the death of Christ may get possession of you. And as often as ye eat, and as often as ye drink, do this in remembrance of Him, of what He was and what He can make you to be. Show forth the Lord's death until He come. God grant that each time you partake of the Lord's Supper, it may increasingly become the power of Christ's death in your spirit and life!

Just two words in conclusion. You may say, "Ought not the Communion to be a feast of joy and gladness?" It ought to be. But you think, "What you speak is dark and depressing." Ah no, brother, it is not; my message is one of resurrection joy. Where is resurrection joy to be had but at the grave of Jesus? Sink into the death of Jesus; carry about His dying in your inmost heart. Strike the roots of your being deep into the grave of Jesus and become nothing, so the joy of God and the resurrection of life shall dwell in you. It is not depressing to hear of death with Jesus; it is our joy and gladness that there is a way open for us out of self and its power, into the life of Jesus himself.

And then the other thought I want to give you is this: Oh, be not anxious about how you will be able to realize all these elements of the death of Christ in your life! When your body is in a healthy state, you spend your half-hour in taking breakfast or lunch, and then your work is done. God has ordered everything so that the assimilation goes on quietly without any effort on your part and without your noticing it. You rise from the table and go to your work; you spend hours in business and never think again about what is going on in your blood to strengthen your bones and muscles. The assimilation of the food is a work of infinite importance, but it goes on quietly, surely, without thought or effort. Even so, when you come to feed upon the broken body and shed blood, quietly and restfully trust Jesus, by His Holy Spirit, to make it real in you. The eating is your work; the inward assimilation is God's work. Just open up your whole being and say, "Lord, one favor above all others—the chief of Thy blessings! Oh, for the power of Thy death in my life!"

I know there are Christians who fear that in our days (there is indeed too much reason for such fear) the Church of Christ knows too little of His crucifixion, the fellowship of His suffering —rejection and separation from everything that is of the world and the natural life. Oh, believer, trust Christ to teach you; yield yourself to Him. Feed much upon His death. He will give you life out of death. He will, in divine power, be your life. And then, as each one seeks fellowship with the crucified Christ, we shall all have fellowship one with another. Praise God! We shall all have fellowship in one bread and prove that we are one body. Nearness to Christ will draw us nearer to each other.

We said in the beginning that the food was the life. Let it be so now. We have been fed with heavenly bread; let our lives be very heavenly. God help us, brothers and sisters! Let us lead heavenly lives; let us, in the death of Jesus, die to the spirit of the world and live the heavenly life. He will do it for us. We have not eaten of this bread each alone, but all together—one bread. Let all hearts overflow in love to each other. Let us pray today, and unceasingly, the prayer that God would bind all His children throughout the world in the bond of the love of Christ, and of His Holy Spirit. Let us so pass through this world, showing forth the death of the Lord "until he come." He is coming in His glory. But until He come, let us show forth His first coming—His death for the world and victory over sin. God help us! Amen.

"The Table of the Lord is a golden link, uniting the two great facts of the Bible—that fact of history, the first advent of Jesus Christ, and that fact of prophecy, His second coming again. The Table of the Lord is retrospective: it takes our minds back to the Cross—we are to 'shew forth his death.' And it is prospective: 'till He come.' Thus, the two ends of our own salvation are united together by this Table of Memorial. We have the first end of salvation now; we are waiting for its final end—the glorious consummation. Like the stars in the heavens, which speak and yet there is no audible voice, the dumb elements of bread and wine speak to our hearts today. And, like Mohammed's fabled coffin, our souls are kept in equipoise by the exercise of memory and hope."—Rev. Geo. C. Needham

"Wherefore, holy brethren, partakers of the heavenly calling, consider the Apostle and High Priest of our profession, Christ Jesus" (Heb. 3:1).